Note to Parents

Here is a collection of stories and activities especially for rainy days—including games to play, toys to make, and even some interesting things to do with thunder and lightning and raindrops!

Preschoolers will especially enjoy listening to the stories, poems, and riddles. They will need your help with directions for the activities, and occasionally with projects that require cutting or sewing. The Jiminy Cricket symbol appears with any project that may require adult help. Older children will enjoy reading the stories themselves, and will be able to handle most projects on their own.

Games and projects use materials that can be found in the home—often items that are usually discarded, such as boxes, odd socks, and cardboard tubes from paper towel rolls. Any items that you might have to buy are inexpensive and easy to find.

Of course, this book can't make the rain go away—but it can help your child turn a rainy day into a day full of fun.

ISBN 0-7166-2900-3
Library of Congress Catalog Card No. 83-51332

It's Raining,
It's Pouring!

Bad-Weather Fundays

Published by
World Book Encyclopedia, Inc.
a Scott Fetzer company
Chicago

The Seven-Day House-Stretcher

Rainy weather usually didn't bother the Seven Dwarfs. In fact, they liked the rain. But one Monday morning when they woke up, it was raining so hard that they could hardly see the trees or the path through the forest. They couldn't even go to work.

The Dwarfs took turns looking out the window—but there wasn't much to see. They took turns playing checkers—but after a while, they grew tired of checkers. Grumpy grumbled. Sneezy sneezed. Sleepy fell asleep in his chair—and snored.

Finally Happy decided to pop some popcorn over the fire. But the first POP was too much for Grumpy! "All this noise!" he sputtered. "Sneezy sneezing and Sleepy snoring and now Pappy hopping corn—I mean, Happy popping corn. A body can't think in this little place. We need a bigger house!" He moved his checker game to the farthest, darkest corner and sat there with his hands over his ears—grumbling, of course.

Tuesday it rained even harder, and Grumpy was even grumpier. All he would talk about was building a bigger house.

"Come on, Grumpy," Doc said. "This house has always been just right for us."

"It *isn't* just right," Grumpy grumped. "It's too small, and we're all in each other's way."

Just then, there was a soft tap-tap-tap at the door. "I'll see who it is," said Doc. He opened the door—and there were a mother deer and her fawn, dripping wet and shivering.

"Goodness," Doc said. "You can't stay out in this rain. Come in and get dry." The animals clip-clopped into the warm room.

"What did I tell you?" Grumpy muttered. "This house is too small. Before you know it, we'll need a house-stretcher to make it bigger." But everyone, even Grumpy, moved over to make room for the deer.

On Wednesday, with the wind still blowing and the rain pounding the roof, the Dwarfs heard a loud

THUMP at the door. Doc opened it. "Oh, my!" he said. In walked the biggest brown bear he had ever seen, with her two cubs. Of course, they were dripping wet, and the cubs looked very sad and hungry. Doc gave the bears a pot of leftover soup, and they drank it in front of the fire. That evening two clip-clopping deer, three snoring bears, and Seven Dwarfs sat by the fire, toasting their toes—but it was a tight squeeze. Even Happy was beginning to wish that the house could be stretched.

By Thursday, the rain was making everyone grumpy! But when Happy spotted four very wet squirrels clinging to a tree branch—well, he couldn't turn them away. "Come on in, little ones," he called. After all, four little squirrels wouldn't take up *much* more room. But with two clip-clopping deer, three snoring bears, four chattering squirrels, and Seven Dwarfs huddled around the fire, the house seemed very small, indeed.

On Friday, no new visitors came all day. Grumpy had just sighed a big sigh of relief when the Dwarfs heard a soft fluttering at the window. Bashful opened it. The rain blew in, and so did five of Snow White's doves. They perched on the mantel and fluttered their wet feathers—all over Grumpy. They strolled around the Dwarfs' feet, pecking up the crumbs Happy brought them. Now there were two clip-clopping deer, three snoring bears, four chattering squirrels, five fluttering doves, and Seven Dwarfs crowded around the fireplace—and the house seemed smaller than ever!

By Saturday, everyone was tired of the rain. The house was so crowded that it was hard to cook or clean or even play checkers. That night, Sneezy heard a tiny scratching at the door—so tiny that it made his nose itch. "Kerchoo!" he said. "I'll see who's there." Six shivering little rabbits were huddled on the doorstep. "Ah—ah—

7

ah—hop right in! Ah—choo!" Sneezy said. "Dopey, get some towels. We—sniff—have more company."

"What did I tell you?" Grumpy muttered. "Too many folks for this little house. I'm going to bed." And that's what all the Dwarfs finally did, because with two clip-clopping deer, three snoring bears, four chattering squirrels, five fluttering doves, and six hopping rabbits around the fire, there really wasn't much room for the Seven Dwarfs.

When the Dwarfs woke up on Sunday, the sky was blue. "Sunshine!" Happy shouted. "Look, everybody. Beautiful sunshine!"

All the Dwarfs—even Sleepy—tumbled out of their beds. Sure enough, the rain had stopped. The leaves and grass were still wet, but there wasn't a cloud in the sky.

Doc opened the door, and the Seven Dwarfs and all the animals stepped out into the bright, warm sunlight. How wonderful it felt to be outdoors again!

Slowly, the deer, the bears, the squirrels, the doves, and the rabbits began to move off into the forest. Suddenly, everything was very quiet. The Dwarfs went back inside and began to make breakfast. For the first time in days, they had the house all to themselves.

"Why, look how big the house is!" Grumpy said. "I didn't realize we had so much room."

"Hee, hee, hee—I know why," Happy chuckled. "With so many visitors, I'll bet the house *did* stretch!"

And everyone agreed that it really must have happened that way!

Cozy Corners
for Rainy Days

Sometimes, when it rains and rains, the Seven Dwarfs get grumpy—and Grumpy gets even grumpier. But they've found ways to be happy as Happy. They make cozy rainy-day corners for themselves and their favorite things.

Bashful's hideaway is big enough to share with his favorite bear and his favorite books. Bashful spreads an old sheet over a table. For a doorway, he pulls up one side of the sheet.

rug

chair

fishing equipment

Happy goes camping right at home and stays warm and dry. He makes a tent using two chairs, a rope, and an old sheet or blanket.

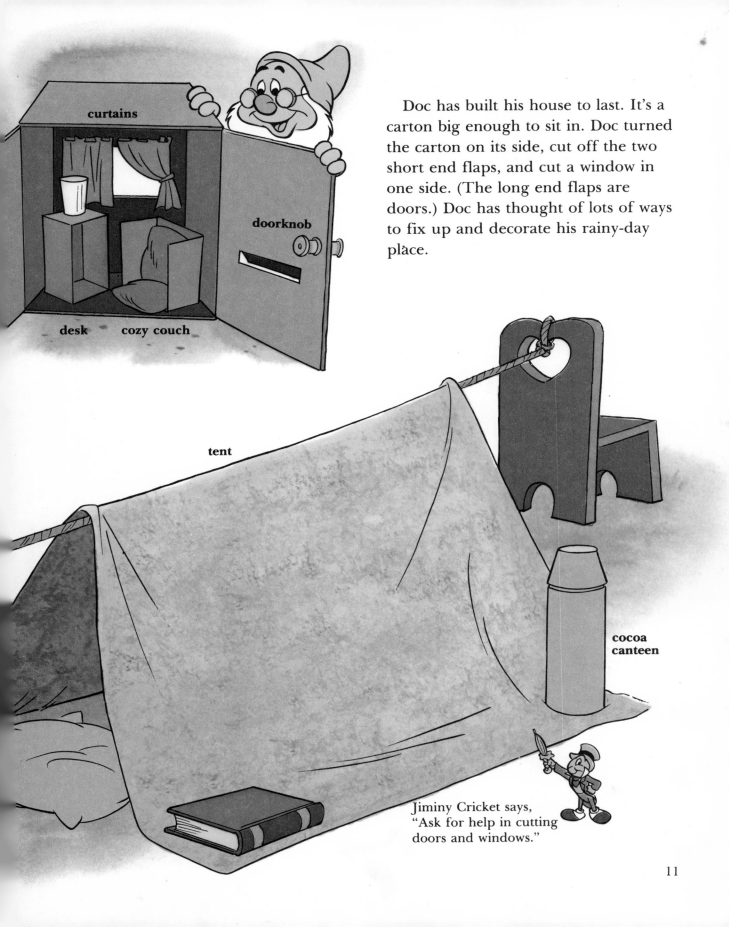

curtains

doorknob

desk   cozy couch

Doc has built his house to last. It's a carton big enough to sit in. Doc turned the carton on its side, cut off the two short end flaps, and cut a window in one side. (The long end flaps are doors.) Doc has thought of lots of ways to fix up and decorate his rainy-day place.

tent

cocoa canteen

Jiminy Cricket says, "Ask for help in cutting doors and windows."

Bright Lights and Dark Shadows

Sometimes on dark, stormy days, the Seven Dwarfs make shadow pictures on the wall. All they do is turn on a lamp in a dark room. They stand between the lamplight and the wall to make shadow pictures.

PEANUTS

Dopey can make a shadow that looks like an elephant. Dopey can make the elephant shadow pick something up with its trunk.

When Doc stands in front of the lamp, everyone looks at the wall and sees a giant rabbit. Doc hops up and down, and the rabbit shadow hops, too.

Bashful doesn't like to stand in front of the lamp, so he makes shadow pictures with his hands. Here are two of his favorites for you to try.

Make an alligator. Hold one hand palm up and lay the other hand, palm down, on top of it. Curl the index finger of your top hand to make the alligator's eye. Keep your palms touching and "clap hands" with just your fingertips to make the alligator's mouth open and close.

Now make a bird. Hold your hands up, with the palms facing you. Cross your wrists and hook your thumbs together to make the bird's head. Wave your fingers back and forth to make the bird fly.

You can have some shadow fun on a stormy day. Just turn on a bright light in a dark room. Stand between the light and the wall. See how many different shadow pictures you can make.

What to Do with a Raindrop

The Dwarfs know that a drippy day is perfect for having fun with raindrops. Bashful likes to paint with them. He starts with a plain white paper plate—not the fancy, plastic-coated kind. Then he dribbles on some paint or food coloring. He lets the raindrops do the rest. When the painting looks the way he likes, he brings it inside to dry.

Even Sleepy stays awake for an exciting downhill water-drop race. He spreads out an old newspaper and makes a "mountain" with tin cans. The slope is a sheet of foil. Sleepy traces paths from top to bottom with the eraser end of a pencil.

Each player dips a pencil in water and shakes off all but one water drop. Players hold their pencils at the top of the mountain. At the count of three, each player shakes a drop of water onto a path. First drop to reach the bottom wins!

Grumpy won't admit it, but he likes to look at flower petals, grains of pepper, and other tiny things through a raindrop magnifier. It makes them look big!

Grumpy cuts a square of cardboard. In the middle, he cuts a circle the size of a quarter. Then he cuts a square of plastic wrap big enough to cover the circle. He tapes the wrap in place.

Next Grumpy dips a pencil in water and gently shakes a drop or two onto the plastic window. He holds the magnifier over whatever he wants to look at.

Grumpy says things are easy to see if he puts them on a sheet of white paper under a bright light. Here are some of the things he looks at:

Jiminy Cricket says, "Ask for help with cutting if you need it."

pencil shavings   **blades of grass**
postage stamps   **crayon drawings**
newspaper pictures   **pennies**
cat hairs   **dollar bills**

Rain, Rain

It's Raining

It's raining, it's pouring,
The old man is snoring;
He went to bed
And bumped his head
And couldn't get up in the morning.

Mother Goose

Rain

Rain on the green grass,
Rain on the tree,
Rain on the housetop,
But not on me.

Mother Goose

Rain

The rain is raining all around,
  It falls on field and tree,
It rains on the umbrellas here,
  And on the ships at sea.

    Robert Louis Stevenson

To the Rain

Rain, rain, go away.
Come again another day,
Little Bashful wants to play.

Rain, rain, go to Spain,
Never show your face again.

    Mother Goose

Pass the Time, Please!

Watching the clock on a rainy day seems to make time go more slowly. So to pass the time, the Seven Dwarfs decided to make a little timer. That way they could watch the time go by—and time their games and stunts, too.

Look at the next page to see how the Dwarfs made their timer. Everybody helped, so it wasn't hard to do.

When the timer was finished, Doc turned it over. Everyone watched while the sand ran down. After a minute, all the sand was in the bottom jar—and Sleepy was sound asleep!

What you'll need

Clean, dry sand
Two identical small spice jars with snap-on
  shaker tops

A watch with a second hand
A cup
Glue

1. Fill one jar with sand and snap on the
   plastic top.

2. Have a friend use the watch to time you
   while you let sand run into the cup. In
   exactly one minute, stop. Empty out the
   leftover sand. You'll need only the sand in
   the cup.

3. Glue the shaker tops together, matching up
   the holes. If glue gets in the holes, poke it
   out with a toothpick.

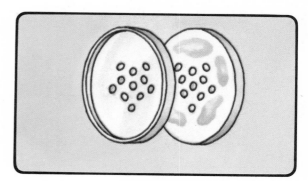

4. Pour the sand back into the jar. When the
   glue is dry, snap the tops and the jars
   together.

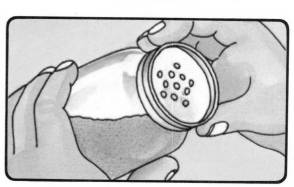

   Here are some one-minute stunts you can
do with your timer.
   1. How many times can you print your
      name before the sand runs out?
   2. How long a string of buttons, beads, or
      macaroni can you make?
   3. How long a chain of paper clips can you
      make?
   4. How many times can you say these
      tongue-twisters?
      baggy khaki jacket
      chocolate chip shops
Can you think of other stunts to try?

Mudball Cookies

The Seven Dwarfs sat around watching the rain for so long that they began to get hungry. Doc decided that he could do something about that. He went into the kitchen and began to get out things he would need to make something good.

Grumpy, who had been outside, wandered into the kitchen. "What are you making, Doc?" he asked. "It looks just like the mud on my shoes."

"I'm making cookies," said Doc. "They may look like mud, but they don't taste like mud."

Grumpy ate a cookie—and almost smiled. "Yum," he said. Then he gave cookies to the other Dwarfs. They liked the cookies, too. Sleepy even stayed awake so that he could eat another one.

You can make mudball cookies, too. Use the same things that Doc used to make his.

What you'll need

Large mixing bowl
1 cup measuring cup
1/2 cup measuring cup

Large mixing spoon
Teaspoon
2 large plates

1 cup uncooked quick oats
1/2 cup broken nut pieces
1/2 cup instant cocoa mix

1/2 cup smooth peanut butter
1/2 cup honey
Graham cracker crumbs

1. Mix oats, nut pieces, and instant cocoa mix together in the large bowl.

2. Add peanut butter and honey. Mix everything in the bowl until it looks like mud.

3. Put graham cracker crumbs in one plate.

4. Take a teaspoon of the cookie mixture at a time. Roll each spoonful in your hands to make a ball.

5. Roll the cookie balls in graham cracker crumbs and pile them on the other plate. Keep your mudball cookies in the refrigerator for snacks or dessert.

Up . . . Down . . . One . . . Two!

At the end of a long, rainy day, some of the Dwarfs were bored. Sleepy was tired of sleeping. Grumpy could hardly stand to be around himself. Bashful didn't say a word—but he thought things were pretty dull. But Happy wasn't bored. He kept busy doing exercises. He thought maybe a few exercises would cheer up the other Dwarfs, too.

"Come on, everyone," said Happy. "Make an airplane. Stretch both arms out to the side. Bend forward. Turn from side to side. Then straighten up."

"Keep your arms stretched out and try to touch your left foot with your right hand," Happy went on. "Then try to touch your right foot with your left hand. Point the other hand toward the ceiling when you bend."

"Now let's do some knee bends," said Happy. "Put your hands on your hips and stand with your feet apart. When I say *down*, bend your knees and squat down. When I say *up*, stand up. Down, up. Down, up."

"Let's do one more," said Happy. "Stand up straight. Put your feet together and raise your arms straight up over your head. Now bend over and try to touch your toes. Don't bend your knees! Try to touch your toes five times."

Trouble at Rainbird River

One morning a strange green bird landed on the windowsill and hopped about excitedly until Doc opened the window. "What's the matter, little bird?" asked Doc. "Why are you so excited?"

"I'm a rainbird," the bird said. "I live on Rainbird River—and my beautiful river has stopped flowing. The water is getting lower and lower. Soon the water will be gone, and the river will be dry!"

"That's strange," said Doc. "We'll have to try to find out what the trouble is."

Doc told the other Dwarfs about the problem. "How could the river dry up?" Happy said. "We've had enough rain to fill ten rivers!"

"More than enough," Grumpy grumbled.

"Maybe something is buh . . . uh . . . ah . . . choo! . . . blocking the river," said Sneezy.

"What do you mean, Sneezy?" Doc asked.

"You know—plugging it up and keeping the water from running," Sneezy said.

"We all crossed the river on Swinging Bridge last week," Doc said. "Nothing was blocking it there."

"I walked up the river to Crystal Falls," Bashful said shyly. "I didn't see anything there."

"I think I know what the trouble is," said Grumpy. "I saw a mother beaver gnawing on a tree up above Crystal Falls. I'll bet she has just built a dam across the narrow part of Rainbird River. And the dam must be stopping the flow of the water. Let's go and ask her to move her dam to a wider part of the river, so the water can flow around it."

Doc and Grumpy set out to find Mother Beaver. And when they found her, they found the problem. She had built her home all the way across the narrow part of the river, just above the waterfall.

Doc told Mother Beaver that Rainbird River had stopped flowing below her dam. "Oh, my," she said. "I do like it here. But if you'll help me move, I'll build a new home in a wider part of the river."

So the Dwarfs helped Mother Beaver tear down the dam. Soon Rainbird River was flowing again.

Just at sunset, as the dwarfs were trudging home, they heard a voice calling from the sky. "Thank you, thank you," it sang. They looked up and saw the rainbird flying back to its home by the river. They never saw the strange green bird again—but they often heard it singing happily among the trees.

Sunshine and Rain

"Ah—choo!" said Sneezy. "Ah—choo! Ah—ah—choo!" After three of Sneezy's loud sneezes, Sleepy was wide awake.

"Now what am I going to do?" asked Sleepy. "You woke me up, and I can't go back to sleep with you sneezing all the time."

"I'm glad you're awake," said Sneezy. "You can stay awake for a while and play my game with me. It's called Sunshine and Rain."

Sleepy liked the game so much that he stayed awake until he and Sneezy finished playing it.

You can play Sneezy's game. First make the playing pieces and number raindrops pictured on page 29.

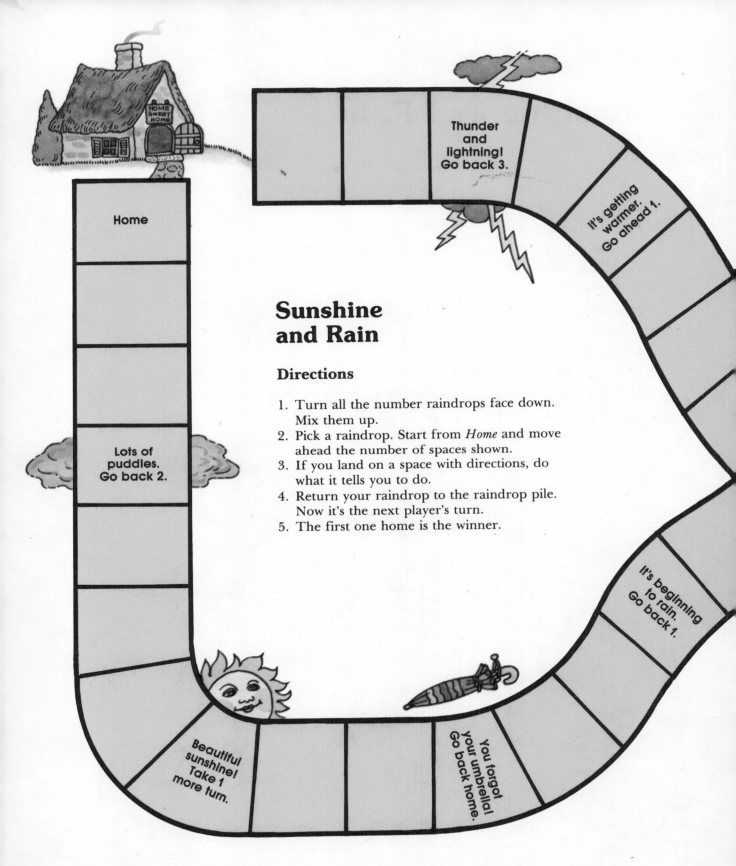

Sunshine and Rain

Directions

1. Turn all the number raindrops face down. Mix them up.
2. Pick a raindrop. Start from *Home* and move ahead the number of spaces shown.
3. If you land on a space with directions, do what it tells you to do.
4. Return your raindrop to the raindrop pile. Now it's the next player's turn.
5. The first one home is the winner.

Home

Thunder and lightning! Go back 3.

It's getting warmer. Go ahead 1.

Lots of puddles. Go back 2.

It's beginning to rain. Go back 1.

Beautiful sunshine! Take 1 more turn.

You forgot your umbrella! Go back home.

28

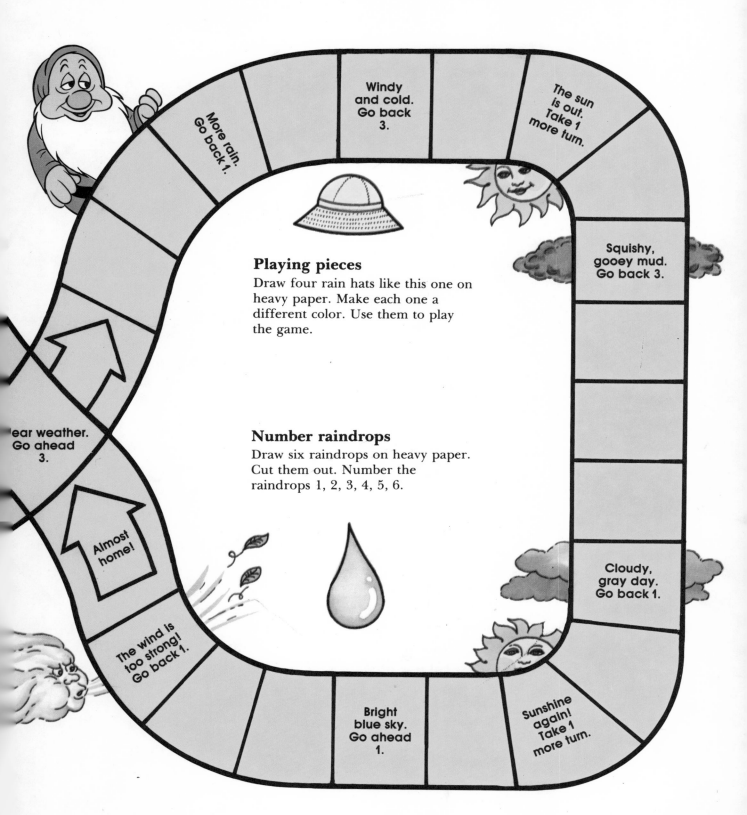

Windy and cold. Go back 3.

The sun is out. Take 1 more turn.

More rain. Go back 1.

Squishy, gooey mud. Go back 3.

Playing pieces

Draw four rain hats like this one on heavy paper. Make each one a different color. Use them to play the game.

Number raindrops

Draw six raindrops on heavy paper. Cut them out. Number the raindrops 1, 2, 3, 4, 5, 6.

ear weather. Go ahead 3.

Almost home!

Cloudy, gray day. Go back 1.

The wind is too strong! Go back 1.

Bright blue sky. Go ahead 1.

Sunshine again! Take 1 more turn.

29

Here's Looking at You!

As you know, Bashful is very shy. He likes to see people—but he doesn't always want people to see him. That's why Bashful has made himself a periscope. He can use the periscope to see what is happening around him. He can use it to see what is going on in another room. And he can even use it to look at things that are out in the rain while he stays nice and dry on the porch.

Bashful has noticed something strange about his periscope. If he holds it straight up and looks into the viewing hole, he sees things right side up. But if he holds it to the side, he sees everything backwards!

You can make a periscope, too. Follow the directions on the next page.

What you'll need
A cardboard tube from a roll of paper towels
Scissors
2 small mirrors
Tape

1. Cut the ends of the tube diagonally, as they are in the picture.

2. Make a light hole at one end of the tube and a viewing hole at the other end. The holes should be in opposite sides.

3. Tape a small mirror to each end of the tube.

4. Your periscope should look like this.

Jiminy Cricket says, "Ask for help in cutting. And be careful when you use your periscope. Mirrors can break!"

A Rainy-Day Book

One rainy day, Sneezy was making something with some old magazines and a pair of scissors. Grumpy wandered in and asked what he was doing. "I'm cutting out pictures of things I like," said Sneezy. "I'm going to use the pictures to make a scrapbook."

Sneezy pointed to the piles of pictures on the table. "Here are some pictures of things I like to eat," he said. "These are pictures of things I like to wear. And those are pictures of toys and games I like."

Then, it happened! Sneezy sneezed, and all the pictures went flying.

"Now you've done it!" said Grumpy. "You're going to wear spaghetti, eat a pair of roller skates, and play with a dish of chocolate pudding. Come on, I'll help you sort your pictures. Just don't sneeze at them again."

You can make a scrapbook like the one Sneezy is making. But be careful! A big pile of pictures is nothing to sneeze at!

What you'll need

Old magazines   Construction paper
Scissors   Yarn
Glue or tape   Yarn needle

Jiminy Cricket says, "Ask for help with cutting and sewing."

1. Cut out pictures of things you like from old magazines. Sort the pictures into groups of things that are alike.

2. Paste each group of pictures on a separate sheet of construction paper.

3. Use two more sheets of construction paper to make covers for your book. Put the pages between the covers.

4. Make two marks on the front cover. This is where you will sew.

5. Thread the needle with about 20 inches (50 centimeters) of yarn.

6. Stick the needle down through the top mark. Leave a long piece of yarn hanging out. Stick the needle up through the bottom mark.

7. Remove the needle and tie the yarn in a bow.

8. Put the title *Things I Like* on your book.

It's Raining Riddles!

What's wetter and sadder-looking than one of the Seven Dwarfs caught in a rainstorm?

All of the Seven Dwarfs caught in a rainstorm.

Why Did Sneezy dive into the river when the storm began?

Snow White told him to stay out of the rain.

What never gets wet when it rains?

A fish—it's always wet.

What can go up a chimney down, but not down a chimney up?

An umbrella.

When you go for a walk in the rain, what should you get wet first?

Your raincoat.

What does a diamond become when it's left in the rain?

Wet.

What did the ground say when it began to rain?

If this goes on for long, my name will be mud!

Beans and Seeds

On rainy days, Dopey liked to make pictures—and pretend that he was a great artist. One rainy day, Dopey saw Bashful going out for a walk in the rain. He wanted to make a picture of Bashful and his big, beautiful umbrella. But he couldn't find his paints anywhere!

Dopey thought and thought—and he finally figured out how to paint without paints.

When the picture was finished, Dopey gave it to Bashful. Bashful was so pleased that he hung the picture right over his bed. That way he could see himself with his big, beautiful umbrella every day, even when it wasn't raining.

Here is the picture Dopey made. His "paints" are beans and seeds that he found in the kitchen.

You can make a bean-and-seed picture, too. You can draw a picture like Dopey's or one of your own. And you can use the same beans and seeds Dopey used, or any other kinds that you have in your kitchen.

Jiminy Cricket says,
"Ask for help with cutting."

What you'll need

Heavy cardboard   Yellow split peas
Dark-colored yarn   Lentils
Glue   Rice
Green split peas   Barley

1. First, draw an outline of Bashful and his umbrella (or a picture of your own) on a piece of cardboard.

2. Spread a little glue along the outline of your picture. Stick the yarn all along the outline.

3. Spread glue on one part of the picture. Cover the sticky part with one kind of beans or seeds.

4. Do the same with the other parts of the picture. Use different kinds of beans or seeds for different parts of the picture.

5. Let the glue dry completely. Now your picture is ready to hang.

Buttons and Beads

While Dopey was making the picture of Bashful and his umbrella, Sleepy woke up. He wanted to find something to do between naps.

Sleepy got out his collection of buttons and beads. He had a whole sock full of them! He emptied the sock. Then he put his hand in the sock, wiggled his fingers, and got a wonderful idea! He would make a sock puppet. His idea kept him so busy that he forgot to go back to sleep.

You can make a sock puppet like the one Sleepy made. After you finish your puppet, you can make up a play for it—or you and your puppet can just have a nice, long talk.

What you'll need

A big, old sock   Needle
Buttons   Thread
Beads   Scissors

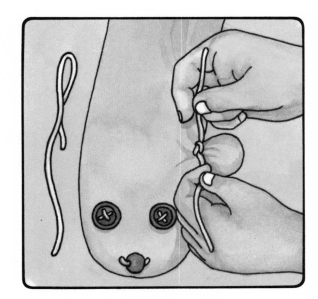

1. Lay the sock flat on a table, with the heel underneath. The toe will be the nose of your puppet. The heel will be the chin.

2. Sew a button in the middle of the toe to make a nose.

3. Sew two buttons above the nose to make eyes.

4. To make an animal puppet, draw some of the sock material together on each side to make ears. Tie thread around the bottom of each ear.

5. Put your hand in the puppet. Stick your fingers in the toe and your thumb in the heel of the sock.

6. Open and close your hand and wiggle your fingers to make your puppet talk, laugh, cry, and do many other things.

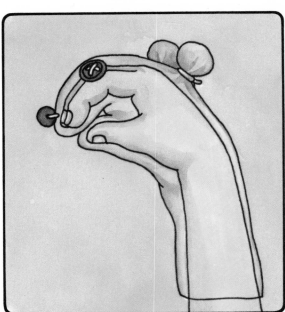

Jiminy Cricket says,
"Ask for help with sewing."

Thunderation!

Early one morning, Happy looked out the window and saw that the sky was very red. "How strange," he thought. Then he remembered an old saying:

Red sky in the morning, shepherd's warning;
Red sky at night, shepherd's delight.

"Look at the red sky, Bashful," said Happy. "A red sky in the morning means that it will rain soon."

"I didn't know about the red sky," said Bashful. "But I do know it will rain, because I just heard thunder. I wonder where it's raining now."

"We can figure out how far away the storm is," said Happy. "The lightning and thunder happen at about the same time. But we hear the thunder later because the sound travels more slowly than the light does. So if

we count the seconds it takes the thunder to get here, we can find out how far away the storm is."

Bashful looked up and saw a flash of lightning. He counted slowly, "One . . . two . . . three. . . ." Fifteen seconds went by before he heard thunder.

Happy said, "Sound travels one mile in five seconds. So if you divide the seconds you counted by five, you'll know how many miles away the storm is."

"That's easy," said Bashful. "It's three miles away."

Happy and Bashful kept on watching and counting. They knew the storm was getting closer, because the time between the lightning and the thunder was getting shorter, and the thunder was getting louder.

Finally, there was a bright flash and a big bang! Grumpy jumped out of bed with his eyes still closed. "Thunderation!" he shouted. "Stop that counting and banging around. Can't anyone get a little sleep around here on a rainy day?"

Jiminy Cricket says, "Sound travels 1 kilometer in 3 seconds. So, to find out how many kilometers away the storm is, divide the seconds you counted by 3."

Inside-Outside Games

The rain had almost stopped. Just a few drops were falling, and the sun was trying to shine. "Hmm," Happy thought. "Why not make a game that we can play inside—and then take outside when the rain stops?" So Happy made a ring toss game.

Happy turned two small paper plates upside down. He taped a bathroom-tissue tube to the bottom of each plate. Then he dropped a few marbles in each tube to keep it from turning over. To make the rings, he cut the centers out of several large, plastic lids.

Doc used his old socks to make
beanbags. First he cut the tops off the
socks. Then he filled each sock foot
with dried beans and sewed it shut. He
made his stitches small, so that the
beans couldn't fall out.

Then Doc made a game for his
beanbags. He painted a big lion face
on a box. Doc cut out the mouth. The
dwarfs played "Feed the Lion" by
throwing beanbags in his mouth.